How To Get Over The Start Line

A Book for People with Anxiety, Their Families and Health Professionals

ALEX EVANS

R Hyp, Dip Hyp CS

CP
THE CHOIR PRESS

First published in the United Kingdom in 2022 by
The Choir Press

ISBN 978-1-78963-314-6

Contents

Acknowledgements

There are many people who have helped and influenced me on my journey. Some I never got the chance to meet in person because they have sadly passed. I studied their work and recordings incessantly when I was creating my therapeutic approach and I often hear their wise voices in my head when I'm speaking to my clients. They are hypnotherapists Dave Elman, Gil Boyne, Jerry Kein and Steve Parkhill.

Others that greatly inspired me were Roy Hunter, Cal Banyan, Gordon Emmerson and Bruce Lipton. I'd also like to acknowledge fellow hypnotherapist Paul Gibson, with whom I've shared much of my therapeutic journey. We've bounced many an idea off of each other trying to make sense of the human mind and why people do what they do.

I'd like to thank my wife, Rachel, who supported my family while I was training, and my inspiration and greatest achievements of my life, my beautiful, talented children, Lily, Joe and Rose. I'd also like to thank my parents and my grandparents for their love and support growing up. When you hear so many stories of challenging childhoods it makes you appreciate when you have a good one.

It takes a lot of courage to talk to a stranger about your worries so I'd also like to also acknowledge my clients for their bravery in sharing their thoughts, feelings and innermost fears.

Introduction

Mental health issues cause a wide range of anxiety disorders including depression, OCD, phobias, PTSD, agoraphobia, psychosomatic pain and illness. For some, the relief from mental anguish is found in the excesses of alcohol, drugs, eating too much or too little, exercising, gambling, self-harm, excess shopping, the list goes on and on. These habits can cause tremendous pain, not only to the sufferers themselves, but to their families, friends and to wider society.

The biggest challenge for anyone suffering from a mental health problem is where and how to begin their healing journey. I'm going to give you another way of looking at how to tackle the mental health problems that cause anxiety. I'll explain how issues are created and why they are maintained. I'll explain why it's so diffcult to stop doing things that we know are clearly bad for us and why it's so diffcult to accept and act on good advice. I'll talk about the function of unhelpful patterns of behaviour and how to tackle bad beliefs.

Most sufferers of mental health problems don't have a clue what's going on inside their mind and why they are behaving in the way they do. Even people who have been in therapy before haven't really had anxiety explained to them so that they understand what's actually going on inside their minds.

Some of you reading this may have been in therapy for a long time but still seem to be going round and round in circles, talking endlessly about the same things with very little progress. I will explain why just talking about your problems with family or in therapy has limited effects.

I will explain to you my approach to addressing anxiety-related issues gained from what I have learned from my personal experiences as a hypnotherapist. This is not a book about hypnotherapy though, it is about understanding your mind and creating the correct mindset to begin your personal journey towards healing. It makes no difference if you are already being helped by a counsellor, analysed by a psychotherapist or attending a CBT (cognitive behavioural therapy) course, the information in this book still applies to you.

I have included an in depth pre-talk that I give to all my clients when they first come to see me, and plenty of the same helpful advise I give during therapy. I'll go into how people get themselves into a pickle and how it's possible to get themselves out of one. I'll also briefly touch on psychosomatic and mind/body illness links to trauma, stress and anxiety.

The information in this book is not only useful to the sufferers of mental anguish, but to those living with or trying to help someone else with a mental health problem. Watching a family member or friend suffering from an anxiety issue can be frightening and confusing. Their problems and behaviours may be beyond your own personal experience and difficult to grasp, but this book will help you to appreciate what's going on within their minds.

By the time you've finished reading this book you should have a better understanding of where anxiety comes from, how its maintained and the correct mental attitude that's needed for tackling the related issues that cause mental health problems. I also believe that health professionals would greatly benefit from reading this book as it explains why much of their good advice falls by the wayside.

I have deliberately kept this book short and resisted waffing and padding it out so that you can read the relevant information as quickly as possible. Even though this book is short there is a lot of important information crammed into it so don't rush through it.

Nobody deserves to suffer from anxiety for their whole lives and it needn't take months or years to move on from, so let's get started straight away.

Foreword

'All healing comes from within.'

Usually, the first port of call for anyone unfortunate enough to find themselves suffering from a mental health issue is their local medical practitioner. The expectations are that they will supply some tablets that'll make all their problems disappear. Sufferers of mental health issues usually extend their worry well into the wee hours of the morning so maybe they'll also be prescribed some pills to knock them out at night too. If they're lucky this combination of tablets will take the edge off the anxiety and see them through their current bumpy patch.

If that doesn't work maybe the next step is to seek out a psychologist, counsellor or a CBT practitioner. Add to that a few self-help books that usually recommend self-acceptance, physical exercise and the practice of mindfulness techniques. That may sort things out but what if it fails and all that happens is a seemingly endless cycle of going round and round in circles? The advice seems to make sense but they just don't seem to be able to take it and end up feeling little or no better than when they started.

Then all that's left is a sad acceptance that 'this is how it's going to be forever' or the so-called 'alternative therapies' like acupuncture, Reiki, homeopathy and hypnotherapy. I put my own profession last because the majority of people who come to see me have tried most of the others already. People who come to see me don't have a clue why they feel like they do, but once the mystery of the minds operation is revealed to them their anxiety seems like a much less scary thing to start dealing with.

You don't need to know the workings of an internal combustion engine to drive a car; in the same way you don't need to know everything about psychology, medicine and the inner functions of the brain to help change unrealistic beliefs and bad habits. I will help unravel the confusing stuff and give you an idea how to move forward.

I began training as a therapist in my early forties. The pressure to learn everything as quickly as possible seemed a daunting task. I found myself drowning in psychology text books trying my best to absorb as much information as quickly as possible. Once I began to work with 'real people' instead of case studies from text books, understanding everything about psychology seemed to be much less important. Most people didn't seem to fit into the boxes that they were supposed to and quite often they didn't behave in the way they were supposed to either. I learned that you can give people new information and advice but they won't necessarily act on it just because you think they should, and trying to impose your ideas on them will only be met by resistance. People will only take on board what makes sense to them so it's vital for them to first understand what's going on inside their mind and why they are behaving in the way they do. In my experience if you have a determined person in front of you, willing to learn, process their past and address their current lives, you can predict a pretty favourable outcome.

I've worked with hundreds of clients with different problems, experiences and beliefs with great success. I've learned and practised many different approaches to therapy on my journey. I have helped many people resolve truly awful things that have happened to them. I'm a firm believer that you can move on and heal from anything with the right help and if pointed in the direction. I have a good idea I'm on the right track with my approach as about 80 per cent of my work comes from client referrals.

One thing I have learned though is that I cannot help everyone, a bitter pill to swallow but the people who I find connection with and follow my guidance seem to get much better. I stand on the shoulders of many amazing therapists who stood on the shoulders of many other amazing therapists before them. Many of these therapists are unrecognised in the field of psychology but I hope that one day their contribution will be recognised.

Changing the habits and beliefs of a lifetime takes effort, practice and the creation of new goals. The empowering thing central to moving on with your life is to take personal responsibility for making those changes. Most people suffering from mental health problems feel out of control or victimised by their thoughts and feelings. I'll explain that it is nearly always their own bad beliefs and habits that are keeping them stuck and it's within their power to change them. Once they get rid of the clutter, alter their thinking and focus on the good in themselves and life things will change quite rapidly for the better.

Acquiring one vital piece of information can be all that's needed to alter a person's thinking. Some may call it a revelation, a realisation or a light bulb moment. I'm hoping that you'll find the information in the pages of this book that will enable you to begin your healing journey. So if you find the subject of mental health issues scary and confusing, read on.

1

The Workings of The Mind

'If you cannot find the answer to your problem it is because you are trying to resolve it by using what you already know.'

We use our belief system to make decisions and navigate our way through life. The frightening thing is that the foundation of our belief system was largely in place by the time we were five years old and comprises of the beliefs of our parents (or carers) and our childish perceptions of life.

The mind is a complicated thing so there are always contradictions however you try to explain it, but I've broken it down to make it simple. Most people say they understand this explanation so get ready, I'm about to get metaphorical.

The mind can operate inside or outside. You can only be in one place at any particular moment. You are either inside with your thoughts and past experiences or outside in the world around you. It may appear that you can be in both places at once but that is because the mind is capable of flicking between the two very quickly, but if you were to freeze time at any moment you'd be either outside or inside. There is no track of time when you're on the inside so whenever you lose large chunks of time, that's usually where you've been. I split the mind into four parts. You have an adult part, an unconscious part, a child part and a man on the door. For argument's sake let's say the adult works in the outside and the child and the automatic work on the inside. In between the outside and the inside you have a man on the door. He is the protector of the inside part of the mind. He's officially known as the 'critical faculty of the mind', but the doorman is easier to remember and describes his job nicely.

The Adult Mind

The adult part of the mind is the most recent part of the mind. It's the clever pre-frontal cortex bit that separates us from the other creatures on this planet. It's the part of the mind that has got us to the top of the food chain and is responsible for the creation of all the weird and wonderful things we surround ourselves with: smart phones, computers, cars, rocket ships etc. We have been clever homo sapiens for approximately 200,000 years or so (unless any more skulls turn up in hidden caves). This clever part of the mind is good at working out how to do things, making good decisions (most of the time) and it works logically. If the adult mind were a computer it could process, at the most, nine bits of information a second and capable of focusing on one thing at a time. Some like to brag about being able to do lots of things at once but those other things are automatic. Even women can only truly concentrate on one thing at a time, sorry ladies.

The Unconscious Mind

Now let's go inside. The unconscious mind was there first! We began our evolutionary journey about 3.5 billion years ago as single cell bacteria and when we became multi-cellular creatures we began developing an unconscious to control our physical functions. Compared to the 200,000-year-old adult mind the automatic mind has had millions of years longer to develop and is therefore, unsurprisingly, more powerful. The unconscious is often referred to as the reptilian part of the brain and is responsible for maintaining life, keeping us safe and continuing the species.

The unconscious mind is involved in operating the 12 functioning systems of the body including the respiratory system, cardiovascular system, endocrine system, lymphatic system, immune system, nervous system, digestive system, urinary system, reproductive system, skeletal system, muscular system and peptide system. It responds to whatever is going on around us 'automatically'. Just watch two people in communication and witness their gesticulations and movement as they respond to each other without conscious thought. As you are reading this you are probably making slight adjustments in your seating, scratching your head, blinking and so on. The unconscious mind is continually monitoring physical sensations in the body, responding to thought and things of interest in the outside world, especially potentially dangerous things. We have a natural proclivity to danger because evolutionary-wise, anything that felt threatening could potentially kill us. The unconscious is very wary of danger for self preservation!

For a person suffering from anxiety-related problems their unconscious mind is constantly on the alert for anything potentially dangerous. Even when they are in a place of safety its still on alert. Anxiety is the unconscious mind's way of preparing us to take action in situations that could potentially cause injury or death, something to be avoided at all cost.

Stored within the unconscious mind are thousands of programs that benefit us and allow us to go about everyday life. At some point in our life we learned how to walk and now it is something we do without thought. There are programs on drinking from cups, opening doors, riding bicycles, driving cars, the list goes on. As well as physical programs there are thousands of mental programs that we use to approach things or get things done stored within the unconscious mind.

If we learn something new and then practise it very soon it becomes an unconscious activity. Most of these programs are useful, keep us safe and enrich our lives, but we can easily adopt bad programs that don't serve us well. Practice makes perfect, so they say, and some people have become experts at feeling depressed or anxious by continually running a bad mental program.

All of our memories are stored within our unconscious mind. Everything that has ever happened to us, that caused an emotion, is deemed worthy of remembering, most especially negative things! When we are threatened by something or something scary happens, the unconscious mind takes note so we can avoid that situation in the future. This is an evolutionary survival tool that's helped us to avoid injury and death and it has worked pretty well up till now. The only problem is, we have developed so quickly as a species evolution hasn't been able to keep up. We feel just as threatened being told off at work by our boss as our ancestors would have 12 thousand years ago coming across a sabre-tooth tiger. The physiology is the same but the threat is not! Other emotional incidents worthy of remembrance include brilliant things that make us happy and also really interesting things. This explains why boring things are diffcult to remember, we feel nothing about them. I bet the subjects you enjoyed at school were much easier to revise for than the subjects you disliked? So every memory has an emotion attached and the easiest ones to remember are the scary ones.

Something else that's interesting is the memories we think about the most, gain in power and importance!

Memories can go all the way back to the womb, believe it or not. At some stage of development you became aware that you were somewhere and hopefully somewhere safe! A little further into your development your hearing came into existence, you could hear your mother's voice, her breathing and her heart beating. You could hear sounds from the outside too as you were contained in a water sack that amplifies sound. You could tell whether those sounds indicated something good or bad by their volume and how your mother reacted to them. So if something emotional happened while you were in the womb there will be a representational memory in the unconscious mind of that incident.

It is estimated that we learn more in the first five years of our life than we do in the rest of our lives. That is because when we are born we have no idea of the world outside or had any experiences in it, we can't even see properly! All we see is black and white from short distances. Distance and colour comes a little later, but when we can see clearly we still have no idea what we're looking at! When we are born we know who our mother is as we've been with her for nine months and have a few memories from the womb. Throw in some genetics that predispose us to behaving in certain ways but other than that we are born blank slates. To survive we have to learn as quickly as possible. Young children are often compared to dry sponges, ready to absorb information quickly and with little question. Experts say that children are capable of proficiently learning three languages by the age of five.

So at five years old the basic foundations of a child's understanding of life and where they fit into it are already formed. They know roughly who they are, who the people surrounding them are and what's right and wrong. That's why those first years of life are so important in the development of a child. If a child is loved, encouraged to explore, learns empathy and feels safe, it has a very strong foundation from which it can grow. If a child is bought up feeling unloved, knowing only criticism and in fear of violence, that will form the foundation of understanding for that child.

Now, just think about how many things you can remember before the age of five, there must be loads eh? Some may say three or four things but most people say nothing! If people do remember stuff before five they tend to be very emotional things, either really good or really bad.

So why can't we remember all of those memories before five years old?

Well it's because the adult mind was in the very early stages of development. If I asked you to tell me what you remember between the ages of five and ten you will recall many more things. If I ask you to tell me what you can remember between ten and sixteen, I bet you could recall tonnes of stuff. So the unconscious mind is also the keeper of all of our memories, even the ones we cannot recall, all the way back before we were born.

Another unconscious function is for self-preservation, often referred to as fight, flight or freeze. If we are faced with danger the unconscious mind tells the body to get ready to respond. Depending on the urgency of the threat there can be either an instant or drawn-out response.

If faced with danger we can freeze and hope the threat passes by, run away or stand and fight. As I mentioned earlier, our remembrance of fearful past events and the subsequent avoidance of things the same or similar has kept us alive as a species for millennia.

Evolutionary-wise, freeze was our first defence to threat when we had nothing to escape or fight with. Predators respond to movement so if we freeze there is less likelihood we'll get noticed. Then when we developed fins we could escape. Those fins turned into legs when we were forced out of the water and then two of those legs turned into arms for fighting.

These forms of self-preservation have kept us alive for millennia and are now unconscious responses to real or even perceived threats. It doesn't really matter if the threats are real or not the physiological response is the same. In 99 per cent of my clients their anxieties are mere perceptions of threat, not actual physical threats.

What we believe to be true is more powerful than what we know to be true which explains why people are scared of things they know they shouldn't be.

Incidentally, the freeze response to danger is responsible for causing many psychological and physiological problems including PTSD, chronic pain and illness. The running away and fighting responses to danger help to discharge the build up of negative energy where as freezing keeps the energy trapped inside through inactivity. It's rather ironic to think our first form of defence now causes us the most problems. I will cover this is more detail in the mind/body section later on in the book.

The Child Mind

The child mind is in charge of emotions, feelings and imagination. If we feel anxious, fearful, happy, sad, guilty, shameful or angry we feel it through the inner child. If the inner child feels safe we feel safe but if something happens to frighten us, like an illness, a loss of someone we love or the loss of a job, the inner child feels unsafe and lets us know about it. Just look at any child's body language and you have an idea how it feels because they wear their feelings on their sleeves.

The child is also responsible for the imagination. If you have a child of your own you'll recognise they have wonderful imaginations. This childlike part of the mind turns words in a fictional book into characters that you know what they look like, scenes or situations that you can imagine and exciting parts where you can't put the book down. It's the part of the mind that makes your heart beat through your chest during the exciting or scary parts of a fictional film, makes you feel angry if someone is wronged, or sad if something bad happens to one of the characters you empathise with. It's not the adult that enjoys fictional things: it knows that the book's made up by the author, in the film nobody died, no one was hard done by, all the stunts were done by stunt people and lots of the background was CGI. It was the child mind that imagined what it would be like if those things were for real. So whenever you're daydreaming, watching or reading fictional media or being creative, you are using the child like part of the mind.

The average adult spends about 70 per cent of their day on the inside part of the mind, planning things, remembering things, working things out, daydreaming, enjoying fictional things. Children spend even longer there as they use their imaginations even more.

So you have the most recent 200,000-year-old adult part of the mind that works out how to do things, deals with logic and generally makes good decisions operating on the outside. Then you have the older, more established unconscious and child part of mind where all of our memories are held, physical patterns of behaviour stored, bodily functions maintained, our fight, flight and freeze responds to danger, the seat of our imagination and emotional responses are housed and the place we spend about 70 per cent of the day on the inside.

Remember I said earlier that the outside adult mind was capable of processing up to nine bits of information a second? Well the mind on the inside that's doing all of that other stuff is capable of processing well over a million bits of information a second!

So when the logical adult mind clashes with the unconscious/ child mind, guess who's going to win? Yes, the inside mind. That explains phobic behaviour and why people do things they know they shouldn't be doing. The adult smoker knows smoking is not good for their health. There's a picture of a diseased part of the body printed on every packet to remind them. They know that if they smoke into older age there is a 50/50 chance that they will acquire one of those horrible diseases pictured on their cigarette packets. They know their breath stinks, their clothes stink, maybe their car and house stinks if they smoke there too. They know all of these things so why do adults smoke? Well adults don't smoke, children smoke!

Usually the smoker learned in childhood that to fit in with their peers, look older, cool or do something dangerously exciting, smoking was the thing to do. Once they got past the terrible taste and smell, smoking became an unconscious activity as it was repeated. Then the pattern-making unconscious mind linked it to everything the child and later on the adult did for recreation: when socialising in pubs and clubs, drinking coffee, after meals, during breaks at college or work, when relaxing. Now we have a cigarette linked to everything good in the smokers life. Quitting smoking is not so much to do with the addiction to nicotine as it is about breaking a habit that's been cemented in the unconscious mind.

The same happens to people who eat too much cake, like me. If the inner mind links feeling good to doing anything, even if it's bad for us, it will keep us doing it. Eating sweet things is linked to celebrations and feeling good. So if we feel bad, what will cheer us up? Cake, of course! It certainly makes me feel better while I'm eating it!

The inner mind has no conscience, that's the role of the adult mind which as we know is not very powerful. Anything we do that's bad for us, even if we recognise it, but can't stop doing has roots in the inner mind. Eventually our bad habit, if practised, will feel as natural as walking, opening a door or drinking from a cup and we'll do it with no conscious thought what so ever.

The adult mind is the 'will power', the child mind is the 'if it feels good let's do it and the unconscious mind is the keeper of habits.

The Man on the Door

In between the adult mind on the outside and unconscious/child mind on the inside there has to be some form of protection mechanism. If there wasn't, people could tell you any old rubbish, you'd accept it as true and end up hurting yourselves or others. This part of the mind is known as the 'critical faculty of the mind'. Think of it as a doorman protecting your inner mind. Incoming information is first checked by the doorman with the belief system to see if it matches what we know to be true from our past experiences. If these ideas or suggestions match, they are allowed in; if they don't, they are rejected. The critical faculty of the mind is part of the unconscious mind.

The doorman is like a computer, opening and closing files appropriate to what is being experienced or even imagined. The doorman is ultimately there to protect you, but if the files being opened contain corruptions or bad beliefs, they will negatively effect your decision making.

People who suffer from phobias for example have a corruption in a particular file in their mind. Every time the file is opened they feel an intense urge to escape. Corruptions don't always have to come from real experiences, they can come from imagined experiences. A child being frightened by a cartoon clown on the TV can cause a fear of clowns in the real world. A person with a phobia of clowns can get on with their lives as long as they don't go near a circus but a person who has a corruption in their file of what they believe to be true about themselves has a much bigger problem because that file is used all of the time.

You may have a friend who you pay compliments to that are true but they just shrug them off. It's unacceptable to them because what you've said doesn't match what they believe to be true about themselves from their belief system.

Maybe you find compliments diffcult to accept, even though there's a part of you that knows that they are true. If so, this is the man on the door in action.

2

The Mind in Operation

'Which wolf do you feed?'

Here are some ideas of how the operation of the mind applies to our thinking and how it causes anxiety. Everything we encounter in life first passes through our man on the door to check if it matches with our beliefs. Everybody has different experiences through out their lives so everyone has their own individual filing cabinet. Trying to put yourself in someone else's shoes is going to be impossible because you are both working from a different filing system. This is why we don't all think and act the same. For some people going on holiday and lying on a beach is a relaxing experience, but for some the idea sounds absolutely awful! Our beliefs come from our perceptions of past experiences. Nearly all phobias are unhelpful and unrealistic but to the sufferer their perception makes them feel that they are real.

We are genetically predisposed too focusing on things that frighten us. We have survived as a species through millions of years of evolution by being cautious and avoiding danger, hence why things that make us fearful are so important. To hold our attention the media predominately uses negative stories. They know that events involving death, fear and misfortune are much more attractive to us than positive ones. But if we are not careful, focusing on bad news can become all consuming and cause anxiety. We have to be careful that negative stories in the news and on social media posts don't paint the world as a terrible place with danger lurking around every corner. Our unconscious attraction to negativity that was once there to protect us from danger is now being manipulated by the media to keep us engaged.

We have to be very careful about how much focus and energy we commit to negative things, for the more we focus on them the more important they become. With practice that focus on negativity begins to feel natural and goes on unnoticed. People suffering from anxiety constantly focus on negative thoughts. They play negative scenarios involving those anxious thoughts over and over in their minds. Before long these thoughts and the accompanying feelings become the main focus in their lives. Chronic pain victims monitor their pain constantly, which soon becomes the most important thing to them. What's interesting is that there are moments in the day when they are distracted and their pain is not noticed. This is evidence of a mind/body connection that can be exploited to help reduce discomfort.

It's very easy to prove the mind/body connection and that our thoughts affect our feelings. If you really focus on a bad thought or memory you will eventually notice an uncomfortable physical change taking place in your body. Your heart may be racing, it may result in a heavy feeling, slight nausea or a churning tummy. Funnily enough, anxious tummies commonly lead to symptoms of IBS. Stress often leads to hypertension; acute childhood traumatic experiences can lead to varied health conditions later in life. These problems often come from too much focus on negative thoughts. Now do the opposite and really focus on a good thought or memory and you will notice a very different change in how you feel. We will explore this in more detail later on in the mind/body chapter.

It's also very important to mind what you predict in the future. If you constantly predict failure it can become a self-fulfilling prophecy that will hamstring you and prevent your success. Failure happens because of your negative prediction, not because it was beyond your capabilities. Anxiety sufferers constantly predict failure and they end up avoiding places and doing certain things not because they are dangerous but because their perception is that they are. How many times have you wound yourself up imagining how awful something will be in your mind but it's turned out to be no big deal or not as bad as you imagined? The inner child part of the mind, like the unconscious part is also evolutionary older than the adult mind and therefore much more powerful so if the adult mind clashes with the child mind, the child will win. All of my clients' adult minds are aware that their behaviour is harming them but their child like part of their minds imagination overpowers it.

If you practice bad thinking for long enough it will eventually become unconscious and you won't even notice you're doing it. If you leave an idea in the mind long enough it will become as familiar as an old friend, cementing itself into the belief system. As we know, our belief system was largely in place by the time we were five years old and much of what we believe to be true comes from others. There is plenty of scope in these early years to pick up some bad beliefs.

Many of us continue to act out harmful beliefs like perfectionism and people pleasing that were created in childhood. These beliefs will remain there until more powerful one's come along and replaces them. The main goal of therapy is to challenge fixed ideas. From experience we know that change is possible because we have been learning new things all our lives and from new information comes the possibility of change. Many things that we once believed were true now we know are not, and we don't believe them anymore.

So how do we begin to approach changing these fixed patterns of behaviour and bad beliefs? First we have to understand what we are dealing with. Every client of mine, no matter what their issue, behaviour or bad belief it makes them feel anxious.

3
What is Anxiety?

'The imagination is more powerful
than what we know is true.'

When the unconscious mind notices something that it views as threatening, it tells the body "get ready, something bad is about to happen" The sympathetic nervous system that encourages action is activated and adrenaline is released into the blood stream speeding up the heart rate. Breathing also increases to get more oxygen into the blood stream. Now, if you're about to be attacked by something you don't need to worry too much about digesting your food, so the blood from the peptide system in the body is diverted to the legs and arms to fight or run away. That's why people who are anxious often report churning stomachs, feeling nauseous, breathing heavily, faster heart rates, heavy legs and tingling finger tips.

Another thing that happens when we feel threatened is the adult mind steps aside and is replaced by the unconscious mind that's in charge of the 'lets get the hell out of Dodge' part of the mind. With the sensible adult mind gone it's very hard to think straight when you're feeling anxious. As I mentioned earlier when I talked about the unconscious mind, you can freeze, run away or fight when you feel threatened by something. At times of heightened anxiety there is a tremendous amount of energy being stored up in the body in readiness to take action. As mentioned earlier the most debilitating response is to freeze, as the other two responses use up a lot of the built-up energy by taking physical action. If you freeze the stored energy has nowhere to go. It dissipates very slowly afterwards causing muscle pains and fatigue, hence why exercise is good during times of anxiety. It helps to dispel that pent up energy. Extreme trauma that results in the freeze response can cause the energy to get locked into the body's limbic system, causing problems like PTSD. This is covered in more detail later on in the mind/body chapter of this book.

The next level up from anxiety is a panic, attack, where escape feels impossible, and is therefore something to be avoided at all costs. The physical feelings during panic attacks mimic heart attacks and many a victim will end up in the A&E department of their local hospital believing they're going to die.

When I started out in therapy my goal was to rid the world of anxiety, but anxiety is actually an essential call to action when we are really threatened by something. Anxiety has kept us alert and away from danger for millennia, protecting us from things that could have killed us. If you live in a war-torn country, anxiety would be keeping your mind alert to potentially life-threatening situations. If you meet an angry snarling dog in the street anxiety would encourage you to do something to avoid getting bitten.

The anxiety I see people for comes from a 'perception' that something bad is going to happen. The threat is not actually real but the inner mind perceives it to be because the situation they find themselves in is similar to a past emotionally charged experience. Most phobic behaviours makes no sense to the adult mind but do to the man on the door, who uses the past to decide what to do in the present.

When people practice anxiety they get really good at it like anything that's repeated. Eventually it goes into the unconscious mind, becomes habituated so that the sufferer does it without thought. Given time the anxiety will continue to spread into other areas of the sufferer's life and get worse. Anxiety just won't go away on its own, it has to be faced up to and dealt with.

I tell my clients when they notice their anxiety to check their surroundings and thoughts with their adult mind to see if they are actually in danger. The answer generally will be no, so take some deep breaths, comfort their inner child by telling it 'You're ok, you're safe.' Because if you can placate the inner child the anxiety will at least be reduced and at best dissipated.

Don't expect to be really good at this straight away, because you are a beginner, but persevere because to get good at something you have to practise. Bear in mind how much energy you've put into following those old anxious thoughts and feelings, so be patient and persist. Remember, even if you get frustrated always be kind to your inner child by treating it as you would a real child, so no self criticism when things get tough!

4
Familiarity

'Safety comes from what is familiar to us, not what is best for us.'

The biggest obstacle standing in the way of change is familiarity. Once a belief is accepted by the unconscious mind it becomes a fixture. Any challenge to a fixed idea will be vigorously defended, even if it's a bad one, so prepare for a battle if your goal is to change fixed beliefs.

Usually bad beliefs come from childhood experiences and get years of compounding before they are recognised as unhelpful. Due to the immaturity of the child and the lack of life experiences to challenge bad beliefs they solidify in the unconscious mind and when re-experienced, compounding occurs making them even more powerful. This is why anxiety never goes away on its own, it just strengthens with repetition over time.

The adult mind may eventually recognise the belief to be a bad one but the familiarity that supports it will continue to fight the challenge of the new idea. Any threat to the old belief will be met with stiff resistance from the more powerful unconscious mind.

A couple of examples of this are people who stay in jobs they hate or people who stay in bad relationships. They know they'd be happier doing something more fulfilling as a job or finding a partner that respects them, but the move from familiarity seems more frightening than staying with what they are used to. This is why it feels unnatural for people to change, because to change is a jump into the unknown.

The adult mind can even become complicit in the maintenance of the bad belief from fear. What if I never get another job or find another partner who'll have me? Maybe this is the best life has to offer so I'd be best to stay here?

How many of you have resisted doing things you know you should do because of the fear that you will be even worse off if you change what your doing?

You may hear this from others, or maybe it's a phrase that you use, 'Why does this always happen to me?' The people who regularly use this phrase are often running a program that is so familiar they don't recognise that it's causing them a problem. Because they run the same bad program, they obviously get the same result but they don't recognise they are the ones making the wrong choices.

For change to happen there must first be an awareness that the way they are thinking and behaving is causing them a problem. Up to the point they will be unaware that there is a problem because their behaviour is so familiar. Have you ever tried pointing out to someone that maybe the cause of their problem is the way they're acting, only to have it thrown aggressively back in your face? You can even supply them with evidence of their foolishness but they will still reject your observations. Once the unconscious mind accepts something as true it becomes a fixed belief to be defended at all cost. This ignoring of facts is called cognitive dissonance and there is plenty of that around at the moment.

Maybe you are approaching life in a way that consistently gets you bad results because of the repetition of bad patterns of behaviour that have become familiar?

The take from this is that 'security comes from what is familiar to us, not from what is best for us'. If we continue to use the same approach the results will be the same. Sometimes people have realisations or lightbulb moments that can change that familiar instantly, but for most change is a slower, more measured thing that takes effort and practice. Unfortunately, sometimes people have to be at rock bottom before they are even ready to look at their own behaviour. Discovering your own part in your downfall can be a very bitter pill to swallow. On the other hand taking responsibility for your part in your past unhappiness is empowering because now you can start to do things differently. You know exactly not what to do because that's what got you into trouble in the first place.

5
Taking Responsibility

'*Become the king of your own castle.*'

Here is a metaphor that I use to make sure that my clients understand our responsibilities during therapy. You could substitute my role for anyone attempting to help a family member or friend. It is essential that everyone in a therapeutic relationship understands their roll to achieve a successful outcome.

I'm taking a walk on the banks of a fast-flowing river. My attention is drawn to a person shouting for help in the middle of the river. Because I'm a person who likes to help, I go and find a ring with a rope tied to it to help pull them in. I throw the ring to the drowning person and tell them to put the ring around their waist. Then I start pulling on the rope to get them in.

It's a fast-flowing river and I'm not strong enough to pull them in on my own so I tell them to start kicking and swimming towards me. With us working together they are soon out of imminent danger. Just before they get to the bank I let go of the rope and encourage them swim the rest of the way on their own. I tell them that If they need me I can always pick up the rope and give them a little more help.

Now here's where things can start to go wrong. If they do nothing to help me pull them in they will remain stuck in the river as I'm not going to be strong enough to pull them in on my own. I'm also going to get really tired doing all the pulling and because it's a fast-flowing river I could even get dragged into the river myself. Then both of us would be drowning in the river, neither able to help each other get out. This is a very common situation to find yourself in if you're trying to help a close family member with a mental health issue. Maybe you are expected to do all the pulling while they do nothing to help. It is your job to support and encourage and you may need to enrol the help of a professional to stop yourself getting dragged into the river in this case.

Another common scenario is when two drowning people try to help each other. They are attracted to each other because of their commonalities but neither has firm footing on the solid ground of the bank. They are both unable to help each other out of the water and they also run the risk of dragging each other down during any challenging times.

My job as a therapist is to support, help resolve past trauma, challenge bad beliefs and encourage new healthy approaches to life. My client's role is to change their thinking, unhelpful habits and anything in their current life that is keeping them stuck. We must both understand and accept our rolls to work effectively together.

It's really important that anyone stuck in the river be aware that all the while they think of themselves as a victim, they will remain there. They may feel perfectly justified to be there because they have had a terrible upbringing or had something awful happened or was done to them, but as long as they hold onto that way of thinking they will remain victims of the river.

Empowerment comes from taking responsibility for the things you have control of. Those things are what you focus on, where you take your thoughts and how much energy you give them. You must recognise that the past is over. The past is there to learn from and use its lessons to protect you in the future, not to repeat and relive every day.

To move forward you will have to address diffcult subjects like unhealthy relationships, jobs or harmful habits. These things are the kicking and swimming towards the shore that create change and get you to firm ground.

If you are the helper and feel that you are getting dragged into the river because the drowning person won't help themselves, you may have to let go of the rope to prevent you getting dragged into the river. If you get dragged in, you are certainly no help to them and now you're drowning too.

Others can help but all healing comes from within. You would be surprised how empowering it feels once you begin swimming back towards the bank instead of waiting for someone to pull you in. Now you are taking charge and releasing yourself from victimhood!

6

Belief Systems

'I think, therefore I am.'

Everyone has their own individual belief system. Belief systems are formed by a combination of the individual's experiences and the beliefs of those who were involved in raising them, these include parents, close family, school teachers and peers (basically anyone the child believes is in authority of them). Because of this, belief systems are more likely to be subjective than true.

Therefore a child is at the mercy of the people raising them and their own ability to be able to process what's going on in their world. Give a young child poor parents or a challenging situation like a divorce to process on their own and it becomes obvious that there is potential to create a bad belief, maybe powerful enough to hamstring that person for life!

Nearly all anxiety-related issues come from either a trauma or a misunderstanding. In my experience these issues usually begin before the age of six years old. Because the adult mind is not very well developed at that age most people don't have access to those early experiences, but they are there, buried deep in the unconscious mind. That is why using hypnotic age-regression techniques are so helpful in my profession.

I must emphasise at this point that problems very often come from a child's misinterpretation of an event, rather than from bad parenting or a terrible trauma. It's not helpful to trawl back through the past trying to find someone to blame because for one thing you run the risk of creating a problem that didn't exist. Also parents and carers don't generally set out to make their children lives miserable so be careful not to play the blame game. As I mentioned earlier, blaming someone else from your past for how you behave today keeps you stuck there and makes it difficult to move on.

Once a belief is practised it becomes familiar and as we know, safety comes from familiarity, not what's best for us. That's why people ignore facts even when the truth stares them in the face

The main reason that people find changing their ways so diffcult is because change involves doing something different. It's taking a jump into the unknown! It's far easier to stick with what is familiar to us than change. Until we start to accept what we believe may not be true and break away from habitual thinking, we will remain stuck in familiarity.

A therapist's goals are to address bad beliefs and help their clients create new ones conducive with happiness. Personally the hardest pill to swallow is not being able to help someone and convince them that it is possible to change. If I cannot get my ideas over in my pre-talk and gain my client's trust I'll lose that client. This book contains a lot of information from my first session, which is why it's called 'how to get over the start line'. If my clients don't believe that change is possible Then Nothing Will Happen During Therapy.

The Fear of Failure

In adulthood failure is believed to be something to be avoided at all cost, but it wasn't always that way. Up to the age of five failure seemed to be perfectly acceptable. We were allowed to mispronounce words, fall over and spill drinks, but the older we got the more unacceptable failure becomes. Failure opened us to criticism and potential embarrassment from our parents, teachers and peers. It's important for us to relearn the value of making mistakes because they allow us to learn and accept others' will also make mistakes too. The fear of failure can lead to the two most harmful traits a person can hold onto: the curse of perfectionism and people pleasing.

The Curse of Perfectionism

The terrible curse of perfectionism can be placed upon children, often by well-meaning parents who only offer praise when the child gets perfect scores. Children can place it upon themselves if they believe they need perfect scores to please their parents or a children who fear criticism can also place the curse upon themselves. The curse then follows the child into adulthood.

The curse of perfectionism can create very successful adults as the drive to succeed is very strong, but it doesn't matter how much success they have or how much money they earn, they could always have done better! The perfectionist becomes their own worst critic. How often have you heard on the news of an incredibly successful person with seemingly everything including fame and money ending their lives feeling they were not enough?

The perfectionist must accept that as part of the imperfect human race they are prone to getting things wrong and making mistakes. A person can only do their best and that's all they can do. It's also pretty obvious that if you repeat doing the same thing there is a very good chance the results will be better the next time. You can always get better at things, so don't beat yourself up that your not an instant expert in everything you do and that sometimes you'll get things wrong.

People Pleasing

People pleasers carry the weight of the world's happiness upon their shoulders. They go out of their way to make everyone else's life easier, often at the expense of their own. Deep down they are the most angry people around because everyone seems to take advantage of their generous behaviour.

People pleasers say yes even when they really mean no and end up doing lots of things they don't want to do, cursing the person they're helping for putting them out and cursing themselves for volunteering to do it. They are happy to accept other people saying no to them but not the other way round.

People pleasing behaviour comes from childhood. If you are bought up by a people-pleasing parent you may pick up the habit or you may acquire it from trying to please a parent that shows little interest in you.

Your selfless work gets little appreciation so you try harder and before you know it it's part of your behaviour.

To move away from people pleasing the sufferer must recognise that they are not responsible for the world's happiness and they are allowed to say no when they mean no! But be prepared, when you begin to say no when you mean no some people don't like it because they are used to your yesses but then you have to ask yourself, 'Are they only friends with me because I always say yes?' If so maybe they're not worthy of your friendship? People who love and care for you will accept your noes as you accept theirs. Once you begin to adopt this new behaviour you'll find that you are doing things you want to do, instead of things you feel you have to do.

Childhood Trauma

To a child a trauma doesn't have to be a terrible car accident or plane crash. It could come from being left alone to cry for an extended period or waking up in car alone because their mum popped into a shop for two minutes and didn't want to disturb their sleep.

There are all kinds of possible ways to traumatise children and most parents have probably unwittingly done them at some time. Whether they turn into significant incidents or not depends largely on the child's ability to process the event but more importantly the frequency of the same or similar events. We must remember that children have limited life experiences so they often need the assistance of a trusted adult to help them process life events. Smacking a child once for a big misdemeanour is unlikely to cause a problem but constant smacking for every little thing can cause a problem.

A lot of childhood trauma comes from being around parents that are trying to deal with their own problems. Children become easy targets for angry adults to vent their frustrations or they are witness to adults violent arguments. Most of these adults are so caught up in their own problems they are oblivious to the effects on their child. Quite often children become the collateral damage of damaged parents trying cope with their own problems.

It's not the size of the trauma as much as the belief that comes from the event that determines how much trouble it causes. A lot of trauma I help people with come from misunderstandings. The child misinterprets what's going on or it's involvement in what's going on. Take divorce for example. Many children take some of the responsibility for their parents' divorce upon themselves or create a belief that relationships are bad or always doomed to fail. These beliefs can cause them to ruin relationships they have in the future as adults. I was working with an anxious lady once who's hair had fallen at 12 years due to the stress caused by an acrimonious parental divorce. Parents need to be mindful of their children when settling their disputes.

Our core beliefs constitute the bedrock of who we are and what we believe to be true today. They are formed at the time when we are the most impressionable and defenceless. We are born into this world without a pre-formed belief system to protect us from bad suggestions. We are basically dry sponges eager to absorb information. The people who were there first are responsible for most of a child's core beliefs and for the majority it's their parents. Parents program children's belief systems using their own. The child does the rest with its juvenile attempts at making sense of the world in which they live. When children go to school their teachers and peers begin to influence their belief system. Many a core belief system was influenced by a bully, a jealous so-called friend or the cruel words of a 'popular kid' at school. Basically anyone who you feel has an authority over you can influence your belief system, especially when you were young and impressionable.

The Jesuits understood how to increase their order and were quoted as saying "give me a boy until he is 7 and I'll show you the man."

7

Where to Look

'We live in the now, learn from the past and move towards the future.'

Here are some areas that can be explored: the past, the present and the future. The past is to learn from, the present is to live in and enjoy and the future should be an exciting place to move towards.

The Past

Some people get themselves in trouble by living their current lives as they have done in the past. They approach life in the same way and make the same mistakes again and again with the same results. You will of course always get the same result if you keep using the same approach! Think of the past as a collaboration of experiences, some to be repeated and some that are never to be repeated.

When things go wrong it is important to run through the situation, assess what happened and learn from it. Was our response appropriate, were certain elements out of our control and what was the outcome? From there we can learn to deal with similar incidents in the future, better armed. Negative events can be wake-up calls, opportunities to grow, or become more resilient and make better decisions in the future. There are many inspirational people who found a new calling or gained their life purpose after experiencing a negative event. For some, bad experiences can be a blessing in disguise, for others they never get past them.

Some try to recreate the good times from the past but forget that they are older, with more experience of life, probably more responsibilities and less innocence. They try to replicate the past but forget they are no longer the same people they were back then.

Some ruminate by replaying every single mistake they have ever made and fantasise how fantastic life would be if they had only made different choices. The truth of the matter is you made the decision with the information you had at the time, not with the hindsight you have now. If I had hindsight I'd have bought lots of houses back in the early nineties, sold them in 2007 and would now be sitting on my boat in the Caribbean!

Maybe you have suffered a trauma or traumas that are persistently on your mind. Are there things that you can't do that you should be able to or are you gripped by fear in certain seemly innocuous situations or do you replay an awful event that terrorises you in your mind? If you are behaving in a way that causes you problems there is usually an event behind it that caused a belief to be created.

Some traumas are directly related to known past events. Some happened so long ago they are not consciously remembered and some events are skimmed over, so seemingly insignificant they do not appear to be traumatic to the adult mind. These early childhood unremembered or seemingly insignificant events cannot always be accessed on your own so you may need some assistance of a professional. Once these events are identified, understood and processed the fear caused by these traumatic experiences can be dispersed.

Bad memories of traumatic incidents fall into two categories: intellectual or emotional. If you can think about a bad memory and talk about it without breaking down then it has been intellectually processed but if you break down, it means that there is still some negative charge attached to it and it is still emotionally unprocessed. Obviously, if the memory is of a loss you will naturally feel sad thinking about it, but if the sadness is overbearing and persists for years it could do with being addressed. If the loss was of someone close and the ending wasn't pleasant and that's all you can focus on then it needs addressing. When you think of someone you've lost the good things about their life and the happy times you spent together should be foremost in your mind. The sum total of a person's life shouldn't be represented by the bad bit at the end and I'm sure they wouldn't want to be remembered like that either.

I have helped many clients with social anxiety who enjoyed not having to socially interact during the Covid lockdowns but then struggled going back to normal life. Their problems with socialising actually existed way before the epidemic, all the back to childhood. The lockdowns were actually 'the straw that broke the camel's back'. Their inner child enjoyed spending all that time at home and kicked up a stink when the adult had to go back into normal life.

If you have located a problem from childhood you have to view it through the child's eyes. Here is an example of how misleading it can be trying to solve problems from childhood using adult reasoning, explaining why using adult logic is not effective in some situations.

Jane is twenty-eight years old and suffers from long term anxiety. She has had anxiety issues for as far back as she remembers and has been in and out of counselling for the last eight years. Even though the anxiety is still in there in the background she feels more in control of it. She is married to a kind man called John who would make a fantastic father. John wants to have children but the mere mention of it makes Jane feel scared and anxious. Unfortunately her fear has begun to affect her relationship with John.

When she was a little girl her father, an alcoholic, used to physically and mentally abuse her and her brother when he was drunk. Her mother never stood up to her father. Jane remembers hiding with her brother from him when he returned from the pub inebriated. On occasions she'd witnessed her father hitting her mother, which was understandably very frightening.

Eventually, her parents divorced when Jane was nineteen years old, two years after Jane had left home. Jane has always been close to her mother and sees her regularly. She sees her father a couple of times a year when she has to. He remarried and is much less angry but still drinks as far as she knows.

On the face of it you might think her father was the problem, but she has already worked through much of the anger and resentment towards him in counselling and has accepted his alcoholism as a major factor in his behaviour. So what's going on with Jane?

While in hypnosis it was revealed that Jane's fears of becoming a parent stemmed from an issue with her mother. Jane's inner child was still very angry with her mother for not protecting her from her father and not leaving him when she was a little girl. This is a very common issue, because at the core of it the child believes the mother should put it's safety over and above everything else. Accompanying Janes unconscious anger towards her mother was a fear that she would be incapable of protecting her own children just like her mother. After resolving the inner child's issues in hypnosis, Janes feelings about motherhood changed and she felt even closer to her own mother. In the next session we did some forgiveness work, mainly centring on her father, the anxiety subsided and now Jane is excited about starting her own family with John. She is going to use her experiences to be a better parent. This is an example of learning from the past and extracting the good from a situation that seemed on the face of it to be only bad.

The Present

It is important to feel secure in your day-to-day life. Many people I see are unhappy in their relationships or they're working in jobs they that hate. Sometimes there is conflict within their family or friendship groups. As I mentioned earlier changing is diffcult because it involves a jump into the unknown. Safety comes from familiarity but if we don't address our current lives, life will continue to disappoint. You can have all the therapy you like but until you address the things in your life that make you feel bad they will continue to trigger your anxiety.

Perceptions of danger also cause people anxiety in their day-to-day lives. Once sufferers realise that most of their anxiety is being generated by imagined thoughts of disaster or failure they can begin to work on them.

Anxiety is there to protect you from real danger but the wrong use of the imagination only causes unnecessary fear. The imagination is actually more powerful that what is real, so if you are using yours to imagine disaster you are going to feel anxious.

So if you feel anxious first stop, check your surroundings for danger, of which you'll almost certainly find none, and tell yourself it's ok, you're safe. If your thoughts are predicting disaster ask yourself how realistic they actually are. You'll find that nearly all of those thoughts are unrealistic and if your disastrous predictions actually come true it's probably because you've hamstrung yourself by expecting them to. In affect they have become self-fulfiling prophesies.

A failed relationship or job loss can leave a person feeling very isolated, especially if they don't have a network of friends to support them. For the lonely, human contact can be found in local groups, church meetings or by attending social activities. Sometimes loneliness can be alleviated with a pet but unfortunately or (fortunately) conversations are usually only one way. There are many organisations dedicated to helping loneliness that can be found on the internet or through your GP and there are of course councillors that can lend a friendly ear and offer advice.

Many people with low self-esteem choose bad partners and friends because they don't feel worthy of being around pleasant, thoughtful people. They have low expectations because they have been programmed by others to believe they are of little value. This belief is purely a perception so if you feel this way have a think about where it came from. Did this belief come from others, or from you misinterpreting your past experiences? Also does your self-talk affirm these bad beliefs?

Whenever you are using negative self-talk be reminded you are saying those things to your own inner child. How is that child supposed to grow in confidence when all it experiences is criticism, anger and resentment? Growth comes from love and support so start being kinder to yourself and take yourself away from people who don't want the best for you. Nurture friendships with the people who are pleased for you when something nice happens in your life, not ones who downplay your success or quickly revert the attention back onto themselves.

Many people are surrounded by friends and family who care for them and offer them encouragement. Unfortunately their mind rejects their kind words and compliments. They reject the love that's being offered and think that people are only saying these things because they have to. Think about how many compliments you reject: they are probably true, so if someone says something nice, thank them. When you open up your heart and really listen to those who love you you'll find that you are actually quite a nice person to know.

It's always easier to blame others than to look inside, but healing has to happen from the inside. Ask yourself this question 'Are you keeping yourself a victim by blaming others?'

Sometimes people are genuinely hit by a string of bad incidents, but others bring misfortune upon themselves. It can be helpful to ask yourself 'Is it bad luck or is it my behaviour that brings about misfortune?'

People who have a string of bad relationships often think of themselves as unlucky in love and say, 'Why do I always get the bad ones?' Quite often a woman raised by an abusive father is subconsciously attracted to abusive men 'like their father'. Women with mothers who were subservient to their husbands often allow their partners to walk all over them as they repeat the behaviour of their mother. Men who were raised by controlling, overbearing mothers marry hen-pecking wives who make their lives a misery. These people are programmed to repeat the lives of their parents because the abuse they face seems normal to them. If you recognise that you are repeating your parents mistakes or maybe a victim of their programming you have a chance to address your behaviour.

The Future

It's important to have an idea of where you want to be and what you want to be in the future. If you don't, you will miss out on opportunities. Just imagining you feeling fit, healthy and happy is a start but the more detailed it is the more focused you can be. If you have nothing to aim for you will miss opportunities so start thinking about what you want in life. Just a picture of you feeling safe, happy and relaxed is a good place to start. Then add some feeling.

Goals change as you grow older. A teenager's goal maybe to get to learn a trade or get into university, a twenty something maybe to get the dream job, a father or mothers goal may be to keep their children safe while they are growing. Many people have a crisis in their midlives where they have reached their goals and are now searching for a new purpose. In my early forties I decided to move away from retail work, which after twenty-five years had become unfulfilling. My original idea was to work with troubled teenagers. I could imagine myself doing it and began a new adventure through counselling and eventually into hypnotherapy. If you'd told me years ago that I'd end up as a hypnotherapist I'd have laughed. At first my goal was to help and this is where it took me.

Once you have that idea of what you want your future to look like the next stage is to start your journey and that's the tough bit. You begin to sift out all the things in your current life that no longer serve a purpose and take steps toward your goal.

Beware, some live too far in the future, waiting for the planets to all align before they do anything. They talk themselves out of moving forward, fearful of failure, helplessly watching the years and opportunities disappear in front of their eyes. To reach your goals you have to just start, even if things aren't perfect, and trust you'll get your dream at some point.

8
Making Changes

'*Knowledge is only potential,
taking action is power.*'

Intention

For people to change, there first must be a recognition that the way they are thinking and behaving is wrong. Then they must be able to create enough energy capable of moving them towards something better. That drive has to be accompanied by an intention to follow through with the necessary changes and succeed.

My own recognition of the power of intention started while I was studying martial arts many years ago. If my mind had no focus during a training session, gains would be made to my fitness but not skill. If I wanted to raise my skill level I would have to focus my mind's intent on achieving that goal to improve.

When I later became an instructor I would encourage my students to work on developing an intention in threatening situations that they would only be pushed only so far and willing defend themselves if necessary. It's amazing how many confrontational situations can be defused by a projection of intent. Once you understand and adopt this idea you will automatically feel more confident. Young children recognise the point where their parent saying no actually means no. A steely glance with intent for most is enough to behave. That is the power of intent in action.

My intention is to help everyone who comes to see me! If my expectations are low then that will surely be felt by my clients. I must create an energetic environment conducive to change and install a confidence in them that is what is going to happen.

Communication isn't only about the words you speak, they must be accompanied by intent for them to be effective. When I say 'I'm going to hypnotise you now,' to my clients, I have to intend and expect it to happen or I will fail. They must feel the intent emanating from me.

The language we use is very important to convey our intent and there are certain words that can be disempowering if used in the wrong context. Below are three words that can prevent us from moving forward. They are Try, Hopefully and But.

Trying is Lying

A very commonly used word in the English language is try. Unfortunately, trying has an inbuilt get-out clause that sets you up for failure because if you fail you can always say 'Well at least I tried.'

So substitute the words 'I'll try' with 'I will' and your intention will change and increase your chances of success, but only if you say it with meaning. If you want someone to do something for you and they say 'I'll try' just push them to say 'I will' and it'll be more likely that they'll follow through. Notice how many times you use the word try in your language, or if you are helping someone else notice how many times they use it.

Hope Means Hopeless

Hope is a lovely sounding word but it's not really an empowering word. Hope implies that something will magically happen out of the blue. Many people live their lives hoping their situations will change but do nothing to change them.

For change to happen you have to do something to make it possible. That brings me back to intent. Changing the phrase 'I hope to get better' to 'I will get better'. That is much more empowering.

Do you remember earlier I said 'All the while you remain a victim you will stay stuck in the river?' Hoping that something will happen will keep you stuck in the river.

The But Word

Everything that comes before the word 'but' is negated. I may ask a new client how they have been over the past week. They might say, 'Oh the first four days were wonderful, I felt fantastic, but on the fifth day I woke up tired and irritable and for the next three days I couldn't get myself together.' The but word completely wiped out the first four fantastic days and left the focus on the three bad days that preceded. Another way of using the but word in the positive is, 'The last three days haven't been great but the first four days were fantastic, I felt wonderful.'

Do you use the 'but' word to wipe out anything good that happens in your life?

Acceptance

We are all victims of our past. Children's belief systems are formed by their experiences and from the teachings of parents, carers, relatives, teachers and from their experiences. That makes everyone slightly different. To coexist peacefully we have to agree to uphold certain values, but outside of them, we have many differences. That's why it's impossible to put yourself in another person's shoes.

What I'm writing makes perfect sense to me but when it gets to your man on the door it has to be compared to your past experiences and belief system so that you can make sense of it. My meaning could easily be misinterpreted by your understanding of what I'm saying. Look at any social media post on the internet and you will see a variety of different opinions being expressed in the comments. Some you'll wholeheartedly agree with and some you'll strongly disagree with. Sometimes the way in which things are said can be confusing and easily misconstrued, often ending in an argument. So we have to accept our differences, make allowances and be flexible or people will always upset us.

Generally people are doing the best they can and have the best intentions. If you are trying to understand someone it helps looking at their past. If your mother was emotionally distant think about how her parents treated her when she was little. If she didn't experience love how was she supposed to show it to you? If you are looking back into the past it's helpful to look at the experiences of those who hurt you to gain an understanding of why they may have behaved in the way they did. This is no way justifies their actions if they hurt you, but maybe explains why.

Understanding your parents' past helps to understand their behaviours and can help remove some of the unfair feelings that cause anger and resentment. Parents don't usually set out to cause their children problems. They are trying to cope with their own issues and unfortunately their children become the collateral damage as I mentioned earlier.

Forgiveness

'*Holding onto anger is like drinking poison and expecting someone else to die.*'

All the while you hold onto negative feelings towards the person who hurt you, you will painfully continue to suffer for what they did. You may have justification for being angry because they did terrible things to you but as long as you hold onto it you take ownership of it.

Generally people think of forgiveness as something that if given, lets someone off the hook, or that to forgive is to forget. Forgetting is not possible because what they did hurt you, but you can learn to depersonalise it and let it go. The forgiveness that heals comes from your recognition that you are no longer prepared to be the keeper of the negative feelings that came from someone else's actions. You are not letting them off the hook, you are refusing to carry around what they did to you.

It's also important to recognise that the person that hurts you the most is the one inside your head. Quite often the perpetrator is no longer around any longer but they still torment you. So when you forgive, all of the forgiveness is actually for you as you're letting the perpetrator in your mind go. If you are unfortunate enough to occasionally see your tormentor, the act of forgiveness stops you from continuing to absorb their negativities. Some people say I need to hold onto that hate because what they did was terrible, but holding onto that anger is bad for your physical and mental health.

It is also equally important to forgive yourself for anything that you may feel you have done to others. We are all members of the imperfect human species and sometimes we make mistakes. Anybody looking back at their own mistakes recognises that if they had been aware of the impact of their decision they'd have made a different choice.

This healing forgiveness can be a diffcult concept for many people to get their heads round. The plots of many popular films are based on revenge as a justification for wrongdoing and we enjoy watching people get their comeuppance but in reality revenge makes you do things that are not of your nature and afterwards you will have to carry the weight of your actions.

Holding onto any negative feelings is no good for your mental and physical health, so let it go! I help people to do this all the time in therapy and it's a life-changing experience when they let go of the negative feelings for people who hurt them with forgiveness.

Your Life is What You Focus on and Search For

The inner mind is goal oriented; it will do everything it can to help you reach your goals. The difference between a happy person and an unhappy person is where they focus their energy. The depressed person goes out into the world looking for the bad and their inner mind, believing that's what they are interested in and helps them find it. They also look for the bad in themselves. Good things happen to depressed people but they either don't notice them or brush quickly over them. They predict everything they do will fail and those thoughts become self-fulfilling prophesies. Their hearts and minds are closed to any good around them. When they come home they sit down and ruminate on past failures, what they should have done, and the unhappy memories. Then they go to sleep with their bad dreams, wake up tired in the morning and repeat. Very soon this way of thinking, acting and behaving has become habitual and they don't recognise they're doing it.

The happy person does exactly the same but their focus is different. They look for the good in themselves, and in the world around them. They predict success in what they do and because their minds are open to the good, they see the opportunities that come their way. When they think back to the past their subconscious mind helps them to recall the good memories. Of course bad things happen to happy people, but they deal with them and go back to looking for the good.

You may have every reason to be unhappy with your life but as long as you place all your attention on the bad that's what your subconscious mind will show you.

Once you recognise the past is gone, begin predicting success, open up your heart and mind to the good in the world, yourself and others, your inner mind's goals will change. It's not easy to change your focus but it is something that you have to work on to move forward.

Redirecting Intrusive Thoughts

You have no control of bad thoughts coming into your head, they just turn up, but you do have control of where you take those thoughts. People invest a lot of time and energy into focusing on negative thoughts. Give them thirty seconds to focus on a negative thought and they've attached another ten negative things to it! Then they practice focusing their attention on those negative thoughts; get really good at it and soon it becomes habitual.

Generally the first thing that people do to try and stop negative thinking is to not think of negative thoughts. This method is always doomed to failure because you can't not think of something without thinking about it first! Here's an example: whatever you do, don't think about a pink elephant on a bike. I know that as soon as you read that a pink elephant on a bike popped into your head.

The first thing to do is to notice when the intrusive thoughts begin. Then stop and tell yourself, 'I know if I continue to focus on these thoughts I'm going to feel terrible and I'm really sick of feeling that way.' Then you take your mind somewhere else or do something that makes you feel good that is completely the opposite. Whatever you place your focus on or do is for you to discover, everyone's opposite is individual to them. You'll probably be bad at this to begin with but with practice you will improve. Once you discover your new focus you just continue to practice until you have created a new habit. This method of re-direction is not running away from your old thoughts, it's facing up to them, seeing them for what they are and choosing to take them in another direction.

Internal Representations

All of us have an internal representation of ourselves, sometimes referred to as our ego. This representation comes from our beliefs about ourselves. Our belief system began forming when we first became aware in the womb. In my line of work many clients in hypnotic regressions go back to very early incidents in childhood that affected their belief system. These incidents are often unavailable to the adult mind as it didn't come into awareness until the age of five years old.

If our child like internal representation is that of a loser, or a fool, or not enough of this or not enough of that, every decision we make will be based on that. Hypochondriacs believe they are ill and spend hours visiting doctors and specialists only to be told that they are fine. They don't believe their diagnosis because it doesn't match their internal belief that something's wrong with them. Our internal representation affects how we feel about ourselves and what we believe is true about the world around us. These beliefs are often not true but purely perceptions.

We learned about 60 per cent of our lifetime's worth of knowledge by the time we are five so the foundation of our belief system was pretty well developed by then. The majority of our belief system came from our parents, the rest from our juvenile attempts at trying to understand and process our experiences.

If a young child has an emotionless mother, an abusive father, experiences a divorce or any major trauma it has to make sense of those experiences with its immature belief system. It's very likely that a child who experiences trauma and is left to their own devices will come to the wrong conclusions about what happened and their part in it. Early beliefs form the bedrock of a child's belief system and those beliefs are carried forward into adulthood where they will continue to think, act and behave with the child's beliefs.

If you recognise that you are acting from a bad belief system you can begin working on changing it. It's not easy because these beliefs have been compounded for years; it involves some reflection on the past and the installation of new much more appropriate and realistic adult beliefs.

When you look back into your past it's not helpful to look for someone or something to blame, as that only keeps you stuck as a victim. Healing comes from acceptance that it was what it was, but that was then and this is now. Life is happening in this moment, the past is to learn from, not to repeat all the habits that make us feel bad.

Once you understand this you can begin on recreating a realistic internal representation of yourself and replace the childish perceptive representation that you've been holding onto. It takes time to form new mental patterns of behaviour so don't expect this to happen overnight and you may need some professional guidance.

It's strange that we accept learning something physical will take practice but expect learning a mental process to be instantaneous. They are exactly the same so accept you are a beginner but the more you practice the better you'll get. Eventually your new thinking habits will become unconscious and the old habits will fade or remain as warnings of behaviours not to repeat.

Imagination

Developing a new internal picture of how you want to be and how you want to feel in the future is really important. If you can't imagine being able to do something, your subconscious mind will be unable to help you achieve it. Close your eyes and imagine a you that can do things you desire. Image how it feels, what you'd look like when you have what you want. Imagine yourself succeeding. When you have done that repeat doing it every day to compound this new you in your subconscious mind. Always use your imagination to create a you that already has what you desire. If you wish or hope for things the message to yourself and the universe is that you don't have them. French psychologist Emile Coue encouraged his clients to repeat the mantra 'every day, in every way I get better and better' to cement the idea into the unconscious mind.

Any artist will tell you that you cannot will the words of a song, a moving poem or a wonderful painting onto paper. These ideas come from the imagination. As we know the child part of the mind is responsible for the imagination and children, as you know, don't always use their imaginations in the best way. People suffering from mental health issues generally use their imaginations to predict disaster or failure. Often their internal image is that of a loser or someone who's not enough of something or a victim of something or a victim of someone else's actions. They live their lives based on that internal image and end up making poor decisions that are backed up by what they already believe. If this way of thinking is continued it gets integrated into their psyche.

The difference between a happy person and a depressed person is their internal image of themselves and their belief about the world in which they live. The mind is working in the same way for both but their focus is different. To think something through requires the use of the imagination so it's important that your internal image is realistic, not a childlike image. People who I see generally have very unrealistic views of themselves, and one of the first things I work with them on is their internal self-image.

It is very important that you work towards accepting your minor faults, forgiving yourself for being imperfect and creating an internal image of the person you are to become instead of using your imagination to focus on everything you hate and fear. Healing comes only from love and it's important to imagine ourselves as a lovable, happy, healthy person so that they can be integrated into the psyche.

Is your internal image of yourself good? If it isn't, begin working on an image of a you that you'd like to be in your mind and how it would feel to be that person. I've been writing parts of this book on notepads and in my head for years but never getting on with it. To finish it I imagined myself talking about it to groups of people, physically selling the book, posting copies and receiving good feedback. That gave me the drive to get started. You cannot achieve anything until you imagine it first and you cannot be the person you would like to be until you create that image of that person first!

Self-Talk

I ask my clients to think about the things they say to themselves in their darkest moments. Then I'd say to them 'If you had a five-year-old child standing in front of you right now, would you say those same things to them?' They are horrified. 'No I could never say those things to a child.'

The problem is when you are saying those things to yourself you are saying them to your own inner child. How is your inner child supposed to feel good about itself, grow and feel confident if all you do is tell it you're not good enough? Always treat yourself with kindness and encouragement. If you want to feel good and grow in confidence, nurture your own inner child, because if it feels safe and supported, so will you.

Finding Your Life Purpose

I read a wonderful book called *Cancer as a Turning Point* by Lawrence Leshan a few years ago. He was a psychologist working with terminally ill cancer patients. He noted that the patients who began doing something meaningful in their life or discovered their life purpose lived between three and five years longer than was expected. Some were frustrated artists who rediscovered unfulfilled dreams and others found volunteering within charities ignited a passion for life. Their newfound passion to find purpose extended their lives.

Life purposes can change throughout our lifetime. Even if you are a little old and grey round the temples you still have a wealth of experience and knowledge to draw from as you move into the next stage of life. Use it to enrich your life and that of others and your happiness and contentment will grow.

My wife and her friends are constantly battling their ages. She says to me, 'Its ok for you because you like being old.' It's true, except for the excessive visits to the loo at night and aching hips. I actually feel more balanced and in touch with myself and the world than I did when I was younger. I've dropped lots of those insecurities that young men carry around like mill stones round their neck.

You may not know what your life purpose is at the moment but if you are doing something that you are passionate about, you are not harming anyone else and its making the world a better place you are moving in the right direction, so just keep going.

When Life Challenges Us

The first thing you have to accept is that there is no place of Nirvana where everything is perfect, and once you get there you stay till you die. Life is one challenge followed by the next and satisfaction comes from overcoming those challenges. When faced with adversity you can let it destroy you or you can work your way through it, learn from it and become stronger. That's where satisfaction comes from.

Sometimes things go wrong because of something we did. Sometimes it's down to others' actions or we were in the wrong place at the wrong time or it was just bad luck. But if you look into any seemingly negative event there is always something positive that you can take from it. You may have to go in with a fine razor blade, but if you look hard enough you will find something that will help add resolution or a lesson that can be taken from it to protect you or someone you love in the future. To some of you this might sound stupid but there are many examples of people who have been through adversity and created something that makes the world a better place. Some people find their life purpose from adversity.

Looking for the Good

Helping people find the good in the bad is something that I help my clients with. Some people with terrible parents give their children the opposite experience and become wonderful parents. They discovered the good in the bad from their childhood. Some, unfortunately, don't learn because they were unable to find the good and repeated the mistakes their own parents made with them.

The world contains many unhappy people who project their unhappiness upon others. If we don't protect ourselves with the understanding that 'they are them and we are us', we risk absorbing their unhappiness. We have a choice to accept their negative words, actions, bad manners, chips on their shoulders, anger with how life has turned out for them, or we can reject them.

Always bear in mind it is not your responsibility to save the world. You can help others if you choose but ultimately, if they are not ready to accept your help, there is nothing you can do. You must accept that you only have control of your actions and must be strong enough yourself before you try to help others. Get your own house in order before attempting to help others or you may find yourself in the river drowning with them.

If we look for the bad in ourselves and in the world it's all we'll find, but if we start to look for the good, it will be predominately what we'll find. To look for the good is to look for love at the end of the day.

Healing comes only from love. Anger, fear and criticism prevents healing from happening. If we approach illness in the same way with the mindset of fighting or battling it will also slow down physical healing. In effect we will be battling ourselves. We need to be kind to ourselves and understanding of others differences.

9
Mind/Body

'*The body's natural setting is towards health.*'

This book wouldn't really be complete without a mention of the mind's influence in the creation and maintenance of chronic pain and illness. I would imagine that many anxiety sufferers reading this book may have a physical symptom that accompanies their mental anguish. To explain how our mind affects the body fully would involve writing another book, but here's an outline.

Cells are influenced by their environment. The cell's environment is influenced by hormones, the nutrients from the food that we eat, the chemicals in the air that we breath and absorb through our skin. Equally as important is the information that is received from the mind's perceptions of the world. These perceptions travel through the nervous system to the cells, therefore for every thought there is a corresponding reaction in the body at a cellular level. This forms the basis of the mind/body connection.

Around about 400 years ago in Europe the practitioners of medicine and the Church came to an agreement to allow the study of human anatomy on the deceased. Up until that time dissecting a human body was a crime against God and punishable by death. The Church were persuaded that the head contained the soul, belonging to God, and the body was purely a vessel to carry the soul. Therefore after death it was acceptable for the practitioners of medicine to use the body for the advancement of medicine. Here began the separation of the mind and body in Western medical science.

For a long time afterwards the body was treated very much like a machine: if something breaks, cut it out and replace it. On the plus side, the medical scientists could really begin to study and understand the workings of the human body. With greater knowledge of the inner workings of the body we now have the ability to test for imbalances in chemical composition and even predict illness before it starts. We have an amazing understanding of the operation of the human body and tremendous advances have been made in the treatment of disease. On the downside, the mind/body connection was largely ignored and labelled unscientific in Western medical practice.

Chronic Pain

Pain is there to protect us from further damage after an injury and is essential for survival. It was originally thought to be controlled by the body but we now know that pain is created and controlled by the brain.

Unfortunately there is still a wide belief by the general public that it isn't. The brain decides on where and how painful something should be. Sometimes the brain creates pain sensations when nothing is damaged, or continues to create pain long after physical healing is complete. So if your doctor says your pain is in your head, they're not saying you're making it up, they're saying that there is no physical need for it to be there. If pain relating to an injury continues after it's needed, more often than not it's because the brain still believes the injury is there. When you injure yourself the pain threshold in that area is lowered to protect it, but it won't always return to its original position on its own even when healing is complete. The brain continues creating pain to restrict movement to protect the old injury site. The threshold can be readjusted by slowly and incrementally pushing through the pain. Doctors and pain clinics help their patients to do this using physiotherapy and by encouraging gentle exercise.

Pain can also be psychosomatic and linked to trauma. Quite often psychosomatic pain is worse than acute pain and lasts far longer. Working through the trauma with a therapist or through self-discovery can remove the unnecessary pain though. Quite often these pains are linked to childhood trauma and are triggered by a current life event. There are specialists who can help with this. A good book that I recommend my clients read before I work with them for chronic pain conditions is one called *The Great Pain Deception* by Steve Ozanich.

If you break your arm you go to the hospital, get a cast fitted so the bones can set and in six weeks it's taken off, voila your arm is healed, but not from the cast! All the cast did was hold the bones in place while the body healed. If you cut yourself you may clean and dress the wound, but it's not that that does the healing, it's the body. Medicine helps but it's the body that heals. All healing comes from the inside, physical and mental.

The Autonomic Nervous System

There are two branches of the autonomic nervous system, the sympathetic and the parasympathetic. If we feel threatened, the sympathetic nervous system is activated to motivate us to take action. The parasympathetic nervous system, on the other hand, when activated helps us to rest and digest our food.

Most chronic pain and chronic illness sufferers' main focus is on fear, created by the pain and worry. This activates their sympathetic nervous system creating anxiety, putting the body into defence mode. Stress hormones are released and resources are redistributed in readiness for an impending attack. Unfortunately the immune system is not seen as important at times of stress, making anxious people more susceptible to illness. So feeling anxious, worrying and being stressed is not good for our health. Pain is reduced and healing occurs when the parasympathetic nervous system is activated. So relaxation, meditation, resolving trauma and reframing problems helps to reduce discomfort and stress. The body moves into health mode, which is conducive to healing.

The Brain

The brain communicates with the endocrine system, the autonomic nervous system, the peptide system and the immune system. It processes information from the outside world and the imaginative world. It helps to decide how painful something should be or if something should hurt or not. Any man watching a football match seeing another getting struck in-between the legs will recognise the uncomfortable feeling that comes with witnessing it. But If you close your eyes and imagine the same thing you'll wince even though its only imagined. Just the thought of it causes an internal reaction. Generally people suffering from chronic pain and chronic illness are using their imagination in a negative way and making themselves feel worse. But you can do the opposite by focusing on the good and using your mind to imagine healing taking place. Hypnotherapists recognise that the imagination is more powerful than what is true and use this in therapy to help people create healing from within themselves.

We know that every thought is reciprocated by a feeling within the body. We use many sayings that substantiate this idea. For example, 'My stomach churns every time I think of that' or 'It makes me shudder to think what could have happened' or 'It broke my heart when I lost my pet'. These prove the mind/body connection.

Metaphysics has broken down many physical ailments to specific traumas and bad beliefs that interestingly seem to be right many more times than they are wrong. The mind/body connection that was once poppycock in the Western world is now irrefutable and there are many studies to support this. Eastern approaches to medicine have always been holistically based and therapies like acupuncture and meditation have been used for thousands of years to aid recovery from illness. Only very recently have they become acceptable and practised in the West.

As I mentioned earlier in the book, the subconscious mind is goal oriented and will give you what you ask. A few years ago broken heart syndrome, where one partner gave up on life after losing their other half, was recognised as a mind/body problem. Why is it not possible that constant worry and stress couldn't lead to IBS or anger and resentment turn into a cancer? But if the mind can create pain and illness it can also take it away. Concentrating your imagination on healing can have surprising results.

Body Memory

There is a lot of evidence on body memory and trauma in relationship to chronic pain and illness. This is where energy remains locked into the connective tissues and organs within the body after a trauma is experienced. A victim can remain frozen in fear and unable to function or unable to repair until the trapped energy has been released. Sufferers of PTSD respond very well to the release of body memory trauma as part of their healing. Massage therapy, physiotherapy, osteopathy, chiropractic therapy, somatic healing, polyvagal therapy and hypnotherapy can be very helpful in releasing trapped energy in the body from trauma. Any masseuse will have had an experience where the manipulation of a certain part of their clients body induces an unexpected emotional response. These unconscious responses are energy releases. Sometimes their client may have an old memory pop into their heads as they are being touched or feel an urge to cry.

Acute Childhood Trauma and Illness

The questionnaire below was formulated in 1994 by Dr Robert Anda, a senior researcher in preventative medicine and Vincent Felitti MD to determine the effects of childhood trauma on the health of adults. It was completed by 17,337 people and it concluded that the higher the score, the more chance there was of developing a health problem. The study has been repeated more recently with similar results. The questionnaire covers the first 18 years of life. It was called the ACE study (Acute Childhood Experiences)

If you want to learn more about how childhood trauma affects physical and mental health Donna Jackson Nakazawa wrote a fantastic book called Childhood Disrupted on the subject that I can highly recommend reading.

If you have been suffering from physical health problems why not take the test to see if your childhood may have had a bearing on your health.

THE ACE QUESTIONNAIRE

1. **Did a parent or other adult in the household often ...**
    Swear at you, insult you, put you down, or humiliate you?
    or
    Act in a way that made you afraid that you might be physically hurt?
    If yes add 1 _____

2. **Did a parent or other adult in the household often ...**
    Push, grab, slap, or throw something at you?
    or
    Ever hit you so hard that you had marks or were injured?
    If yes add 1 _____

3. **Did an adult or person at least 5 years older than you ever ...**
    Touch or fondle you or have you touch their body in a sexual way?
    or
    Try to or actually have oral, anal, or vaginal sex with you?
    If yes add 1 _____

4. **Did you often feel that**
    No one in your family loved you or thought you were important or special?
    or
    Your family didn't look out for each other, feel close to each other, or support each other?
    If yes add 1 _____

5. **Did you often feel that**
    You didn't have enough to eat, had to wear dirty clothes, and had no one to protect you?
    or
    Your parents were too drunk or high to take care of you or take you to the doctor if you needed it?
    If yes add 1 _____

6. **Were your parents ever separated or divorced?**
    If yes enter 1 _____

7.   Was your mother or stepmother:

Often pushed, grabbed, slapped, or had something thrown at her?

or

Sometimes or often kicked, bitten, hit with a fist, or hit with something hard?

or

Ever repeatedly hit over at least a few minutes or threatened with a weapon?

If yes add 1 _____

8.   Did you live with anyone who was a problem drinker or alcoholic or who used street drugs?

If yes add 1 _____

9.   Was a household member depressed or mentally ill or did a household member attempt suicide?

If yes add 1 _____

10.   Did a household member go to prison?

Yes No If yes add 1 _____

Now add up your "Yes" answers: _____ This is your ACE Score.

Statistically, the higher your score the more likely you are to suffer from ill health as an adult. Childhood trauma affects the brain development of children and makes them more prone to anti-social behaviour, depression and anxiety. These issues can continue into adulthood but now add on the increased chances of developing chronic pain, migraine headaches, heart disease, cancer, autoimmune problems, fibromyalgia and many other serious health conditions.

Of course everyone who has experienced childhood trauma doesn't suffer from depression or serious illness, but if you did it's something to consider. Because the changes in our biology from trauma are epigenetic you can work on reversing the damage in therapy by processing the past. Unfortunately only about 2 in 10 people will even consider listening to someone talk about using their mind to help to heal their body in the western world. The evidence is there but mind/body healing is still treated as 'the elephant in the room.'

These ideas form the basis of mind/body healing and offer hope to people suffering from chronic pain and illness. If your mind can create or maintain these issues it can also help undo them and begin to heal.

In reality we are the sum of many things, including body, mind and spirit, and if we wish to achieve wholeness all of these must be taken into consideration if we are to fully heal.

10
Therapy

'Give a man a fish and he'll eat for a day, but teach him to fish and he'll eat for life.'

Most of you will have heard the above saying before and it applies in therapy. The removal of the shackles of victimhood and facing up to the things you most fear the most are the main two things that will set you free. The aim of any good therapist is to help their client achieve those as soon as possible. You might say that's obvious but I've met many people who have been with the same therapist for years and have barely moved on from where they started. Their therapist has, in effect become an accomplice in stopping them from moving on by shielding them from their fears and making them reliant on therapy to function. Most people don't need to be in long term therapy, sometimes all they need is one bit of important information accompanied by the proper guidance to break free.

By now you should have an understanding of how people get themselves into a pickle and how it's possible to get out of one. People can do a lot of work themselves but it's difficult to beat the help from a good therapist. A trained professional will be able to look at things in areas that the public are not aware of or would not have thought to look. Therapists can also help with the processing of the past and the changing of perceptions.

When I began training, people seeking professional help from their medical practitioner were one in four. That didn't include the people (especially men) who avoid asking for help. The cases of mental health issues have risen exponentially since then and we must easily be closer to one in three today. A tiny minority of mental health issues can be classed as mental illnesses that need constant medication. Most mental health sufferers are people who are holding onto bad beliefs from their past, have unresolved trauma or are repeating familiar bad habits that get them into trouble. If resolved these issues would lift their funk and allow them to practice living in the now, start looking for the good in themselves and the world that surrounds them.

Therapy only became popular towards the end of the nineteenth century. Peoples' lives were generally much less complicated than today up to that point and most had little use for psychology. Their therapists were family and friends. The early pioneers of psychology included Doctors like Janet, Nietzsche and Freud. Their observations and ideas formed the basis of modern psychology. Counselling became much more popular in the 1960s when society opened up to the idea that it was ok to talk about your feelings. Today we have approaches like cognitive behavioural therapy (CBT), hypnotherapy, eye movement desensitisation reprocessing (EMDR), emotional freedom techniques (EFT), the list goes on. Some therapists combine some of these therapeutic techniques.

Finding the right therapist is very important as your relationship with them determines much of its success. If you don't like or trust your therapist, it doesn't matter how good they are, your 'man on the door' won't let anything they suggest in.

The expectations of success in therapy are far too low in my opinion, so I wouldn't recommend you go with a therapist that says things like 'You'll probably never get over this' or 'This will take years to sort out' or 'I can, at best teach you how to cope with this problem'. By creating a low expectation of success it puts less pressure on the therapist, but much worse, if you are unfortunate enough to accept these suggestions they will become your expectations and belief.

The focus of therapy should be on discovery, helping people to face up to their fears and changing bad thinking programs. Therapy that involves listening and no input, interposed with 'How did that make you feel' and ending with 'That's all we have time for today, see you same time next week' is not helpful in the long term.

Talking about your problems to someone is very important, but endless talking about the same thing over and over will lead nowhere and all you'll do is go round and round in circles. The constant telling of the same story will only compound your unhappiness and prevent you from moving forward.

My own approach is to establish a therapeutic relationship with my client by gaining trust and creating an expectation of healing. I'll take a brief notation on their past and what beliefs were formed, then I'll explain the mind, how it works and how it's possible to heal and finally get them to agree on our roles in moving forward. It then becomes an organic process where we work with what come up from their subconscious mind in hypnosis. When we make discoveries we'll add understanding, process any trauma, change perceptions and create new patterns of behaviour more conducive to happiness.

A client's responsibility in any therapeutic relationship is to address any problematic areas in their current lives and practice new ways of thinking until they become familiar to them. The client who has a 'I pay you so you make me better' attitude will never be successful as they are taking no responsibility for themselves and as I mentioned before, all healing comes from within.

People must also recognise the relevance of their feelings in therapy and feel safe enough to express them. Every thought we have causes a felt response within the body. Our feelings are linked to our thoughts and any attempt to suppress them will only push them even deeper inside. If you are unable to cry or show your anger that pent up negative energy may be expressed in explosions of emotion at inappropriate times, or fester away and cause bitterness and resentment. Even numbness or a lack of feeling has meaning and should not to be ignored by you or your therapist.

Negative stuff from the past can't be swallowed, buried or forgotten, however hard you try. At some point it will rear up its ugly head but with the right help these things can be processed and healed from. Any form of help that avoids facing up to and processing the past is doing a disservice in my view and is only going to make the situation worse. I've come across many therapists who are uncomfortable when their clients express their emotions and do everything they can to avoid them feeling them. Their therapeutic style of avoidance may sound very attractive because no one wants to really reopen all that crap that they've spent their whole life suppressing. Once again, any therapist who uses avoidance of emotion methods becomes complicit in keeping the person they are trying to help trapped.

So phone round and speak to a few therapists to get a feel of who you like, and don't be afraid to ask questions. Better still are to get recommendations from people who have been through successful therapy.

11

If All Else Fails

'Be tenacious.'

Generally people find themselves in a much better place when they begin addressing their issues, both in their past and in their current lives. The things that they've processed make the past easier to reflect on and they can see things for what they really were. If they address their current lives by stopping doing the things they hated and doing more of the things they've been putting off, it will bring about a feeling of empowerment.

If all their issues have not been addressed they will have more limited success though. That's why it's useful to have professional help in these cases. Sometimes when starting a new life, issues that were not in awareness during their therapeutic transformation emerge. That's why it's important to have the knowledge and tools to deal with them if they arise. If people don't have the resources to protect themselves in the future the next life challenge may end up flooring them. If you have an understanding of how the mind works and you're in touch with your feelings you'll recognise any negative emotional shifts in the future and know when its time to seek help if needs be.

The most common reason for a person not to move on is that they do not address the things in their current life that trigger their anxiety. This includes going back to jobs they hate, staying with abusive partners and continuing with the original negative thinking patterns that have got them into trouble in the past. The comfort of familiarity can be difficult to resist and it can take a lot of effort to create new patterns of behaviour.

So what if problems still exist after extensive therapy and changes of lifestyle? Either they or their therapist have been working in the wrong areas or their behaviour gives their subconscious something that it craves. That something is called a secondary gain.

Secondary Gain

Secondary gain is where the rewards of maintaining a seemingly destructive habit outweighs any form of positive change. The adult mind is often not conscious of this problem because it is hidden deep within the unconscious/child mind on the inside.

I may ask my clients if there are any advantages to suffering from anxiety or being disabled by their pain or illness? Are there any things they hated doing before their problem that they will have to go back to if they found resolution? Do they get more attention now than they used to because of their condition? Sometimes this line of questioning can seem a little uncomfortable, but the subconscious mind is trying to protect them from either a perceived danger or fill an unmet need for love and attention. The unconscious mind's goal is to protect, even if the behaviour is harmful. Phobic behaviour is usually pretty unhelpful to your adult part but your unconscious/child part believes it's necessary for survival. It always works in the positive.

I worked with a lady once who had social anxiety accompanied by a back ache. I saw her three times and helped her to resolve some self-esteem issues but things weren't moving forward as fast as I would have expected. She had always been physically active and used to enjoy social engagements. She had no recollection of injuring her back; it seemed to come from nowhere.

She had a full-time job that she hated but retirement was on the horizon in a year or so. It turned out that her husband was a bit of a traditionalist, shall we say. He did nothing round the house to help her and when he came home from work sat straight in front of the TV waiting for his supper to be served. She didn't feel appreciated and resented his attitude towards helping her. He justified his behaviour as he was the main bread winner in the relationship. Her anxiety started at work and was so bad she had to take time off sick. Then came the back problem!

Because of the pain her husband took over the hoovering, any awkward household tasks that involved bending over and took her shopping to lift the bags into the car.

When made aware of her possible secondary gain she was then faced with a difficult choice. The prospect of overcoming her anxiety and back ache would mean that everything would go back to the way it was before. She'd go back to the job she hated full time and her husband would go back to his old ways and stop helping her. She politely declined to continue with therapy after that discovery, probably deciding the anxiety and backache weren't so bad after all.

I have also met people whose anxiety defines them and some have integrated it into their psyche. They call it 'my anxiety'. They've said it to themselves so many times that they now own it. It really is not part of the human condition to feel anxious without a threat to life, so please don't start calling 'my anxiety'. Start saying things like 'I feel anxious when I do X' or 'When I'm in this situation it makes me feel anxious'. These statements are more likely to give you perspective and open to finding a solution.

12

Exercise in Self Exploration

'*The answers lie within the feeling mind.*'

The following exercise is to give you an idea of the areas that you could benefit from exploring further. I have deliberately not included probing questions about the past as they can be misleading without the guidance of a professional.

Choose a quiet time and place, turn off phones, lock out pets etc. to do this exercise. You may choose to have someone you trust read out the questions to enable you to focus your attention on your feelings. I'd advise sitting in a comfortable chair or lying down.

Stay with each question for a while and see if any feelings come up. If you become emotional allow the feelings to flow. Every emotion is valid and indicates how the child feels. If you feel like crying let the tears flow. Why you are crying might not make any sense in the moment but will act as a release and you'll feel much better afterwards. If you have anyone with you they should encourage you to release your emotions, not help you stuff them back inside.

Remember emotional problems lie within the child mind, not the logical adult mind. If you feel a resistance or a numbness rather than an emotion it is also valid and should be explored. Run through every question, even if you don't think it applies to you. My clients are wrong eight times out of ten what their deep down issue is because they are viewing their life using the adult mind and seeing it through the adult eyes, not the childs.

1. Do you feel in control of your life?

2. Are there things that you can't do that you feel you should be able? If yes, what are they?

3. Are you gripped by anxiety or fear in certain seemly innocuous situations? If yes, what situations?

4. Do you replay an awful event that terrorises you to think of over and over in your mind?

5. Do you constantly run through negative experiences in your mind and torment yourself with thoughts of what you should have done differently?

6. Do you constantly use the phrase 'Why does it always happen to me?' If so what always happens to you?

7. Do you use the past as something to learn from or do you feel like you keep re-living it?

8. Are there times or things you do that make you feel unsafe in your day-to-day life?

9. Are there things in your current situation at home or work that if changed would relieve your stress?

10. Do you feel loved and have someone to love?

11. Do you feel accepted or worthy of acceptance?

12. Do you constantly criticise yourself?

13. Do you reject compliments from others?

14. Does your behaviour push people away from you?

15. Do you surround yourself with people who make you feel good about yourself?

16. Do you like your job, or do you do it just to pay the bills?

17. Does your job contribute to and make the world a better place?

18. Are you a perfectionist? Is nothing you do ever good enough?

19. Do you worry about getting things wrong or fear criticism?

20. Do you feel that you are always last on the list?

21. Do you feel that you are responsible for making everyone around you happy or solving their problems for them?

22. Do you find yourself volunteering to do things you don't really want to do?

23. Do you worry about what people think of you?

24. Do you assume everyone thinks badly of you?

25. Do you compare yourself with others and come up short?

26. Does everyone else's life look better than yours?

27. Do you expect things to go wrong all of the time?

28. Do you feel like a victim of your past and can't break free from it?

29. Do you feel stuck and can't work out how to get moving?

30. Have you been waiting for something to happen for a long time?

31. Do you get into a lot of arguments or find yourself bumping into every obstacle placed in front of you?

32. Do you feel angry, fearful, guilty, shameful a lot of the time?

33. Are you waiting for an apology from someone who may have betrayed you?

34. Do you feel like you're living on a knife edge waiting for something to go wrong?

35. Do you spend hours watching TV, flicking through YouTube, playing video games to avoid getting on with life?

36. Do you have unrealistic expectations that set you up for failure?

37. Do you use the word 'try' a lot in your life?

Now you should have some more specific ideas of the areas to focus on. If you had someone help you ask them for some feedback on what they noticed. In a quiet moment you could write down some of your thoughts and feelings about what came up. If you do this just write down what comes into your head with no checking of grammar or spelling. You might be surprised how much comes out.

If you decide to seek professional help you'll have narrowed down the areas that most likely need to be addressed with your therapist or counsellor.

13

In Closing

'The unenlightened are destined to repeat the mistakes of the past and guarantee their own misery.'

Generally the last place people look for healing is within but that is ultimately where it comes from. I hope that by now you recognise the importance of taking control of what you focus on and what you predict. If you focus on the bad and predict failure you will only make yourself feel worse and remain stuck. If you focus on the good and predict success you'll feel much better and have much more success.

Looking outside of yourself for someone or something to blame for your circumstances will only prolong suffering. Demanding or expecting others to do it for you will keep you trapped as a victim of an outside force. Doctors, therapists, friends and family can help but they can't do it for you. You can make a person laugh and smile but you can't make them happy, because happiness comes from within. Your healing comes from within.

As uncomfortable as it might be, you cannot grow unless you look back at times of discomfort or hardship with a mind that's open to learning. We often learn the most when things go wrong because it forces us to reassess, learn and adapt. The inability or refusal to assess the past leaves open the chances of history repeating its self. The consequences of not reflecting and learning are sufferance through repeating the same mistakes. Let go of the past and the people who hurt you. Learn from the bad moments and forgive yourself for your past mistakes. Recognise yourself as a member of an imperfect species that makes mistakes and gets things wrong sometimes. Healing comes from facing up to your mistakes, seeing them for what they were, processing and learning from them.

Continually going back with hindsight is useless as we were different people with less experience of life back then. We must accept we did the best we could with the information that we had at the time, not with the information we have now. If we were aware that our actions would have caused such distress we would of course have taken a different path. We have to content ourselves that we are part of an imperfect species living in an imperfect world, much of which we have no control of, and we will make mistakes sometimes. The only thing we have control of is us in the here and now.

If you are trying to help a loved one, remember you are not their therapist! You already have an established relationship with that person, so don't try to take on the role of a therapist because you will fail! They will see you as a parent or a friend so stick to your role in supporting. Helping someone by enlightening them with the truth can be a double-edged sword because if you challenge you risk offence but if you don't they will remain ignorant of their own behaviour. Your observations will probably be met by stiff opposition and be seen as criticism, so prepare yourself for that.

Be kind to yourself. Never talk to yourself with angry words, criticism or scorn. Encourage your inner child with support, love and forgiveness. If your inner child feels supported you will feel safe. Use your imagination to predict success and allow yourself to be a beginner when you do anything new. This will give you the confidence to achieve anything you desire.

Recognise that it is usually unrealistic perceptions that lead to anxiety disorders but they can be changed because they are self-generated. Recognise the past doesn't have to be your future and your future is yet to be written by you.

Use you imagination to create success. If you work on creating a good internal image of yourself and imagine yourself succeeding it gives the inner mind a goal. Then the decisions that you make are based on what you want, not on what you fear.

We should always remain humble in the recognition that it is not possible to know everything. If we are open to learning and experiencing new things we will be changed in some way. You cannot unlearn or forget your past experiences and even when terrible things happen it is possible to learn something from them. Sometimes you might have to look at them through the lens of a microscope to find that piece of information or the lesson that will help you in the future, but it is there somewhere. The bad thing that happened to you will help to protect you or your loved ones in the future.

You learn the most when things don't go the way you expect because afterwards it gives you the opportunity to assess what happened so you don't repeat them in the future. Learning from bad experiences creates resiliency and strength, so use what you learn to adjust your thinking.

You may have to wait for the good to come from the bad because you are not ready or in possession of all the information you need to fully process the situation, so be patient. Sometimes people who have been involved in terrible tragedy are spurred on to raise money or awareness to help others in similar situations. They become empowered by their new circumstances.

Remember, your beliefs about yourself, what you think you deserve and how you act come from your early programming. The quality of that programming will determine how you perceive life. Poor-quality programming can create unrealistic perceptions that cause problems, but those perceptions are not based on reality. If you change your perceptions of yourself and the world that surrounds you life will change.

The only thing that you have control of in this world is you. You cannot make the world change to suit you and if you sit around waiting nothing will happen. Every journey begins with a step. Then you just keep going and before long, with focus and determination, you'll have an unstoppable momentum that will move you towards the happiness you deserve.

Finally, 'you are not alone'. If you feel lost its because you haven't found your life purpose yet. You are capable of wonderful things and there are many kind people out there that care and who are happy to help, so don't be afraid to ask.

About Me

From a young age I remember finding it easy to talk to strangers. People seem to find it easy to discus their problems with me and I've found myself strangely attracted to people who want to talk about their problems. My journey into therapy began with a counselling course after working for twenty-five years in my wife's family business with my father and brother-in-law.

I graduated from college at nineteen years old and went travelling to Canada, Egypt and Israel. I lived in Israel on a Kibbutz for a year and a half as a working volunteer. When I came home I worked for a bathroom distribution firm before meeting my future wife, eventually joining her in the family business. Our business was selling tools, models and kites. I loved selling kites the most and we sold a lot! The thing I loved the most about selling was working out the customers' needs and desires and matching them up with the right product. They would often come back and talk about what a wonderful time they'd had. That was the most satisfying part for me.

Twenty-five years later and me in my early forties, I started to think about how I'd like to end my working life. I'd always liked to help people, so off on a counselling course I went. Counselling wasn't quite right for me so I changed tack slightly and became a neuro-linguistic programming practitioner with the guidance of John Plester. Straight after that I moved into the field of hypnotherapy and earned myself a diploma in hypnotherapy and counselling skills. I then studied to be a hypnotist with Jonathan Chase and became a registered hypnotist with the Academy of Hypnotic Arts. I've been on quite a few interesting courses, including gut-directed hypnotherapy for IBS, studied the Dave Elman hypnotherapy approach, hypnotherapy for cancer, pain relief and child birth. I've also extensively studied the work of Gil Boyne, Gerry Kein and Steve Parkhill.

I now run a full-time practice in my home town of Norwich in the UK. I specialise in the resolution of childhood trauma and work with anxiety, panic attacks, PTSD, fears, phobias, OCD, chronic pain, chronic illness and many other related mental health issues.